by DICK SADLEIR

BOOK ONE - CONTENTS

© 1968 B. Feldman & Co. Ltd.

First Published as Strum-a-Song book 1. This edition published 1993.

© International Music Publications Limited, Southend Road, Woodford Green, Essex IG8 8HN, England.

FOREWORD

Easy Guitar Sing-along is a guitar song book rather than an instruction manual. It differs from other song books because the melodies are written in keys which are comfortable and easy for beginners. In consequence, without musical knowledge, the beginner can play right away.

Though the volume is a song book rather than a guitar tutor many correspondents have asked for the inclusion of tuning instructions and hints on fingering.

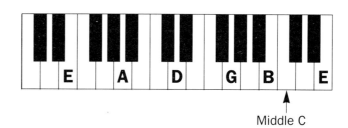

Middle C

The easiest way to tune the Guitar is with a pitch pipe (six little 'pan pipes' each tuned to one of the Guitar strings) obtainable from any music store. Alternatively tune each string to the relevant note on the piano. Middle C is beside the lock on the keyboard.

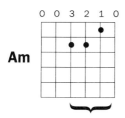

Am

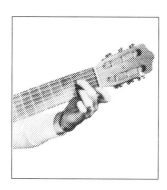

Chords in this book are played from "gate" diagrams. The vertical lines indicate the strings when the guitar is held facing the player. The horizontal lines are the metal "frets" which make the half tone divisions. In the diagram opposite the first string is marked "O" . . or open. This means the full sounding length of the string and the left hand is not used. On the second string the figure "1" indicates that the first finger is used to "stop" the string at the first fret. On diagrams in this book the first four strings are bracketed. These are the notes for a strum chord. Strum across all four with the first finger tip, the thumb or plectrum. Later you will adopt the picking style in which the bars strings are plucked with the thumb and the top three strings with the first three fingers.

To produce a clean "buzz-free" tone, stop the string just behind the required fret and square the finger at the first joint so that the TIP touches. You will soon find that it is accuracy of fingering. . not pressure. . which produces a clean tone. Keep the hand in the position seen in the photograph.

TWO CHORD TUNES

With these two chords you can accompany lots of tunes; there are fifteen in the next few pages! Strum on the first four strings (bracketed) at this stage

G

D7

FRERE JACQUES (Round)

Are you sleep-ing, Are you wak-ing, Bro-ther John, Bro-ther John
G   G   G   G

Ring the bell for morn-ing, Ring the bell for morn-ing, Ding, dong, ding! Ding, dong, ding!
G   G   G   G

BOBBY SHAFTOE

Bob-by Shaf-toe's gone to sea,___ Sil-ver buck-les on his knee,___
G   G   D7   D7

He'll come back and mar-ry me,___ Bon-ny Bob-by Shaf-toe.
G   G   D7   G

Bob-by Shaf-toe's bright and fair, comb-ing down his yel-low hair,
G   G   D7   D7

He's my ain for ev-er mair, Bon-ny Bob-by Shaf-toe.
G   G   D7   G

CLEMENTINE

Clem-en-ti-na, Clem-en-ti-na, Oh, my dar-ling Clem-en-
G   G   G

-tine, Thou art lost and gone for ev-er, Oh, my dar-ling Clem-en-tine.
D7   D7   G   D7   G

POLLY WOLLY DOODLE

LONDON BRIDGE

OH WHERE HAS MY LITTLE DOG GONE

LA CUCARACHA

Come and sing La Cu-ca - ra - cha,   Cel-e - brate in song and sto - ry,
G   D7

All a - bout La Cu-ca - ra - cha,   raise your voice to him in glo - ry,
                                          G

he was a might-y war - rior Surging forth to ev - 'ry bat - tle,_
                                       D7

But he ran in-to a cat's paw,   Lost two legs with-out a rat - tle. __
                                       G

La Cu-ca - ra - cha, La Cu-ca - ra - cha,   He cannot walk any more,   'Cos he has
G

two legs, yes on - ly two legs,   just two legs in-stead of four.
D7   G

DOWN IN THE VALLEY

Down in the val - ly, val - ley so low. __   Hang your head
    G - - G - - G - -   D7 - - D7 - -

ov - er, Hear the wind blow. __   Writ - ing this let - ter,
D7 - - D7 - - D7 - -   G - - G - -   G - - G - -

con - tain - ing lines, __   Ans - wer my ques - tion, Will you be mine?
G - - D7 - - D7 - -   D7 - - D7 - - D7 - - G

6

ONE MAN WENT TO MOW

One man went to mow, went to mow a mead - dow,__
G - - - G - D7 -

One man and his dog, went to mow a mead-ow.__ Two men went to mow,
D7 - - - D7 - G - G - - -

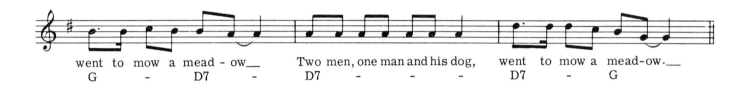

went to mow a mead - ow__ Two men, one man and his dog, went to mow a mead-ow.__
G - D7 - D7 - - - D7 - G

LITTLE BO PEEP

Lit - tle Bo Peep has lost her sheep, and does - n't know where to find them.
G G D7 G G G D7

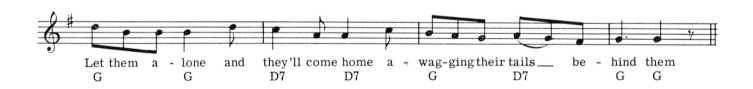

Let them a - lone and they'll come home a - wag-ging their tails__ be - hind them
G G D7 D7 G D7 G G

BOYS AND GIRLS COME OUT TO PLAY

Boys and girls come out to play, No more work at school to - day,
G D7 G D7 G

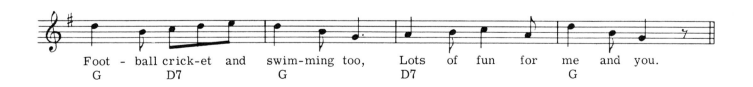

Foot - ball crick-et and swim-ming too, Lots of fun for me and you.
G D7 G D7 G

MUSIC FOR THE GUITAR

You have played guitar chords from diagrams.

G B E

Let us write these chords in musical notation. First, at (A) we set down the open strings of the guitar.

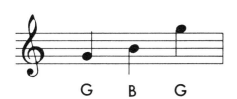

G B G

Next, the chord of G which needs only the third finger on the first string. Memorise the note names.

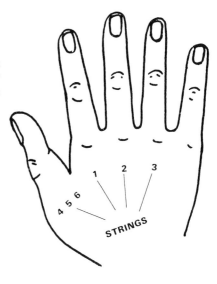

A C F♯

The D7 chord introduces three new note names. F sharp, C and A.

G C E

Lift two fingers and you have the new chord of C.   In the tunes which follow all three chords will be used.

We have been strumming the strings, now let us improve the accompaniment by plucking or picking them with the finger tips of the right hand. The first three fingers do the picking. The thumb is used for the heavy bass strings. When picking with the finger tips try not to hook the strings up.   The movement is as if you laid your finger tips on the table and drew them towards your thumb. The thumb strikes down. To simplify the accompaniment at this stage some players may pluck the chords on the first three strings whilst others play the bass notes.

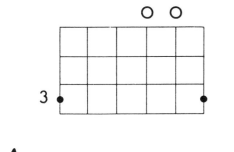

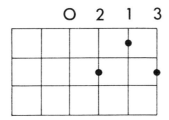

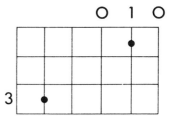

g G d D7 c C

SWING LOW, SWEET CHARIOT

Swing low, sweet char - i - ot ___ Com-in' for to car - ry me home,
G   C   G   D7

Swing low, sweet char - i - ot ___ Com-in' for to car - ry me home.
G   C   G   D7   G

I looked ov-er Jor - dan an' what did I see, ___ Comin' for to car-ry me home, A
G   C   D7   G   D7

band _ of an - gels com - in' af - ter me ___ Com-in' for to car - ry me home.
G   C   G   D7   G

SARIE MARAIS

I'm far far a-way from my Sar-ie Marais, But I'll soon be with her once more, It
G   C   D7   G

was by the Mooi Ri - ver Val-ley that sad day, I left her to go to the war. Oh
              C   D7   G

take me back to the old Trans - val, That's where I long to be, ___ I
C   G   D7

left my lit - tle Sar-ie where the meal-ies grow, Just by the green thorn tree, And
G   C   D   G

I'll be there to meet her where I loved her so, down by the green thorn tree. Oh tree.
                C   D7   G   G

9

THE SAINTS

TWINKLE, TWINKLE LITTLE STAR

BLUE TAIL FLY

THE OLD GREY MARE

Oh, the old grey mare she ain't what she used to be, Ain't what she used to be,
G   **D7**

Ain't what she used to be, the old grey mare she ain't what she used to be
G

man - y long years a - go   Man-y long years a -
D7   **G**   **G**   **C**

go.   Man-y long years a - go. The old grey mare she
G   **G**   **C**   **G**   **G**

ain't what she used to be, Man - y long years a - go.
             D7   **G**

CHIAPANECAS (Pronounced 'Chop-an-ay-cas')

Come and sing with us,___ Come and dance with us,___ To this Mex-i-can
    G   **G**   **G**   **G**   **G**

tune Chia - pan - e - cas___ Clap your hands and sing___ Let your voi - ces ring,
G   **D7**   **D7**   **D7**   **D7**   **D7**

With this gay lit - tle tune Chia -pan - e -cas___ Sing Chia-pan- e - cas, Aye,
D7   **D7**   **D7**   **G**   **G**   **G**   **G**

aye, (clap) (clap) Sing Chia-pan-e - cas Aye, aye, (clap) (clap) Sing Chia-pan-
D7   **D7**   **D7**   **G**   **G**

-e - cas, Aye, aye, (clap) (clap) Sing Chia-pan - e - cas Aye, aye, (clap) (clap)
G   **D7**   **D7**   **D7**   **G**

GOOD NIGHT LADIES

GIMME DAT OL' TIME RELIGION

I WISH I WAS SINGLE AGAIN

I wish I was sin - gle a - gain _____ I
G   G   G   G

wish I was sin - gle a - gain, _____ Oh,
G   G   D7   D7

when I was sin - gle I had mon - ey to jin - gle, I
G   G   C   C

wish I was sin - gle a - gain.
D7   D7   G   G

NEW CHORD

If we learn one more chord we
can play in the Key of C.
This simple chord is called G7.

G7

BUFFALO GALS

I was walk - ing down the street, down the street, down the street, A
C   C   G7   C

pret - ty girl I chanced to meet un - der the sil - v'ry moon.
C   C   G7   C

Buf - fa - lo gals won't you come out to - night, Come out to-night, Come out to - night,
C   C   G7   C

Buf - fa - lo gals won't you come out to-night, And dance by the light of the moon.
C   C   G7   C

COMIN' ROUND THE MOUNTAIN

She'll   be   com - in' round   the   moun - tain   when   she   comes,_____
G   -   -   -   G   -   -   -   G   -   -   -

_   She'll be   com - in' round the   moun-tain when she   comes_____   She'll be
G   -   -   G   -   -   -   G   -   -   -   D7 -   -   -   D7 -   -   -

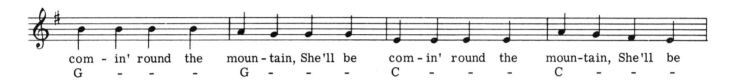

com - in' round   the   moun - tain, She'll be   com - in' round   the   moun-tain, She'll be
G   -   -   -   G   -   -   -   C   -   -   -   C   -   -   -

com - in' round   the   moun - tain   when   she   comes._____
G   -   -   -   D7 -   -   -   G

TWO MORE CHORDS

In preparation for the key of D, look at the key chord D, and its Dominant, A7.

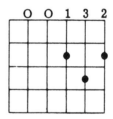

D

Keep the left hand nails cut short, and square the fingers at the first joint so that the TIPS come down behind the required frets.

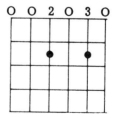

A7

ON TOP OF OLD SMOKY

On top of old Smo - ky, _____ All cov - ered in
D - - G - - G - - G - - G - -

snow, _____ I lost my true lov -
D - - D - D - - D - - A7 - -

- er _____ For court - ing too slow. On
A7 - - A7 - - A7 - - D - - D - D - -

Here is another new and effective chord on the guitar -
A minor.

The small letter "m" is added to the capital as a symbol
for the minor chord.

The fifth and sixth open strings belong to this chord.

O O 3 2 1 O

Am

HEB'N HEB'N (I got shoes)

I got shoes, You got shoes, All God's children got - a shoes.
G - - - G - - - G - - - G - - -

when I get to Heav'n gon - na put on my shoes, Gon-na walk all ov - er God's
G - - - Am - - - G C -

Heav'n. Heav'n, Hea-v'n, Ev - 'ry bod - y talk - in 'bout
G G D7 G G

Heav'n ain't goin' there Heav'n, Heav'n, Gon-na walk all ov - er God's Heav'n.
Am G D7 G C G

16

LI'L LIZA JANE

MY BONNIE

THE FOGGY DEW

When I was a bach'lor I lived all a-lone, I worked at the wea-vers trade, And the
G   C   D   G

on-ly on-ly thing that I did that's wrong was too woo a fair young maid. I
C   D7   G

wooed her in the win-ter time, And in___ the sum-mer too, And the
D7   G   D7   G

on-ly, on-ly thing that I did that was wrong was to keep her from the foggy fog-gy dew.
G   C   D7   G

RED RIVER VALLEY

From this val-ley they say you are go-ing,___ We will miss your bright
G - - D7 - - G - - G - - G

eyes and sweet smile,___ For they say you are tak-ing the sun-shine___
G - - D7 - - D7 - - G - - G7 - - C -

that bright-ens our path-way a-while. Come
C - G - - D7 - - G - - -

sit by my side if you love me,___ Do not hast-en to
C - - C - - G - G - - G - -

bid me a-dieu, But re-mem-ber the Red Ri-ver
A7 - - D7 - - - G - - G7 -

val-ley,___ And the girl that has loved you so true.___
C - C - - G - D7 - - G - - -

I GAVE MY LOVE A CHERRY

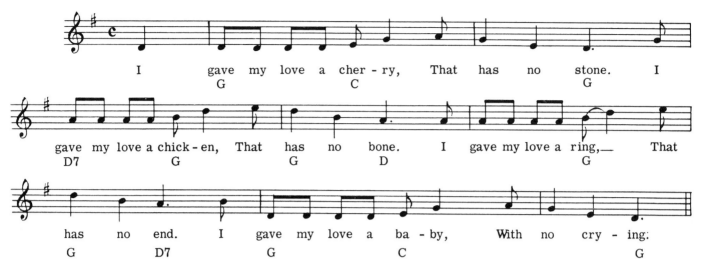

I gave my love a cher-ry, That has no stone. I
G   C   G

gave my love a chick-en, That has no bone. I gave my love a ring,__ That
D7   G   G   D   G

has no end. I gave my love a ba-by, With no cry-ing:
G   D7   G   C   G

How can there be a cherry,   A cherry when it's blooming,
That has no stone?   It has no stone.
How can there be a chicken,   A chicken when it's peeping,
That has no bone?   Has no bone.
How can there be a ring,   A ring when it's rolling,
That has no end?   Has no end.
How can there be a baby,   A baby when it's sleeping,
With no crying?   There's no crying.

HOME ON THE RANGE

Oh give me a home where the buff-a-loe roam, And the
G   -   -   G   -   -   C   -   -   C   -   -

deer and the an-te-lope play,_____ Where nev-er is
G   -   -   A7   -   -   D7   -   -   D7   -   -   G   -   -

heard a dis-cour-a-ging word, And the skies are not cloud-y or
G   -   -   C   -   -   C   -   -   G   -   -   D7   -   -

grey._____ Home, home on the range,_____ Where the
G   -   -   G   -   D7   -   -   G   -   G   -

deer and the an-te-lope play._____ Where nev-er is heard a dis-
G   -   -   A7   -   -   D7   -   -   -   G   -   G   -   -

cour-a-ging word and the skies are not cloud-y or grey._____
C   -   -   C   -   -   G   -   -   D7   -   -   G   -   -   -

OH DEAR WHAT CAN THE MATTER BE?

He prom - ised to buy me a beau - ti - ful fair - ing, A gay bit of
C   C   C   C   G7

lace that the girls are all wear - ing, He prom - ised to bring me a bunch of blue
G7   G7   G7   C   C   C

rib - bons to tie up my bon - ny brown hair._____ Oh, Dear
C   G7   G7   C   C   C   C

what can the mat - ter be, Oh, Dear what can the mat - ter be,
C   C   G7   G7   G7   G7

Oh, Dear what can the mat - ter be, Johnny's so long at the fair.
C   C   C   C   G7   G7   C   C

BLOW THE MAN DOWN

Blow the man down bul - lies, Blow the man down, Heigh ho
C   C   C   C   C   C

blow the man down, We'll blow the man down bul - lies, Blow the man
G7   G7   G7   G7   G7

down, Give us some time to blow the man down.
G7   G7   G7   C   C

BILLY BOY

Oh,___ Where have you been, Bil - ly Boy, Bil - ly Boy, Oh___
C   C

Where have you been char - ming Bil - ly. I have been to seek a wife she's the
C   G7   G7

dar - ling of my life, She's a young thing and can - not leave her moth - er.
C   C   G7   C

A NEW TYPE OF CHORD

Here is a chord in which one finger makes two notes.

The first finger, at the first fret, makes two notes, F (1st string) and C (2nd string).

The finger must be laid flat across the two strings behind the first fret, this is a little difficult at first but you will soon find it easy.

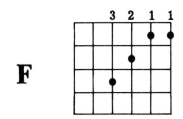

F

TAVERN IN THE TOWN

There is a tav-ern in the town, in the town, And there my
C   C   C   C   C

true love sits him down, sits him down and__ drinks his ale mid laughter_____
C   G7   G7   C   C   F

free, And nev - er, nev-er thinks of me. Fare thee well for I must
F   G7   G7   C   C   G7

leave thee do not let the part - ing grieve thee but re - mem-ber that the best of friends must
G7   C   C   G7   G7

part, must part A - dieu, kind friend a - dieu, a - dieu, a - dieu, a - dieu I
C   F   C   C   C   C   C

can no long - er stay with you, stay with you__ I will hang my harp on a
C   C   G7   G7   C   C

weep-ing wil - low tree, And may the world go well with thee!
F   F   G7   G7   C   C

LITTLE BROWN JUG

My wife and I live all a-lone, In a lit-tle log hut we call our own, And
C   F   G7   C

she likes tea and I like rum, Bet-ween us we have lots of fun.
C   F   G7   C

Ha, ha, ha, Hee, hee, hee, Lit-tle brown jug how I love thee!
C   F   G7   C

Ha, ha, ha, Hee, hee, hee, Lit-tle brown jug how I love thee!
C   F   G7   **C**

CAMPTOWN RACES

De Camptown dan-dies sing dis song, Doo-dah, doo-dah, De
C   C   G7   G7

Camp-town race track, five miles long, Dah doo-dah day!
C   C   G7   C

Gwine to ride all night, Gwine to ride all day, I
C   C   F   C

bet my mon-ey on de bob-tail nag, Some-bod-y bet on de bay.
C   C   G7   C

LAVENDER'S BLUE

Lav-en-der's blue dil-ly dal-ly, Lav-en-der's green,
C   F

When you are King Dil-ly, Dal-ly, I shall be Queen.
C   G7   C

THE YELLOW ROSE OF TEXAS

There's a yel - low rose of Tex - as, I'm go - ing there to see, No
C C C

oth - er cow - boy knows her, No - bod - y on - ly me. She
C G7 G7

cried so when I left her, It like to broke her heart, And
C C C

if we ev - er meet a - gain, We nev - er more will part.
G7 C C G7 C

She's the sweet-est rose of col - our, A fel - low ev - er knew, Her
C C C C

eyes are bright as dia - monds, They spark - le like the dew. You can
C D7 G7 G7

talk a - bout your dear - est maids and sing of Ro - sy Lee, But the
C C C C

Yel - low rose of Tex - as, Beats the belles of Ten - ne - see.
G7 C C G7 C

SWEET BETSY FROM PIKE

Oh do you re-mem-ber sweet Bet-sy from Pike, who
crossed the big moun-tains with her broth-er Ike, With
two yoke of ox-en, a big yel-low dog, a
tall Shang-hai roos-ter and one spot-ted dog.
Hoo-dle dang, fol-de di-do, Hoo-dle dang, fol-de do.

MINOR CHORDS

Minor chords have a plaintive sound but music based on minor chords is not always sad in effect.

The lively sea shanty below uses two minor chords; A minor which you already know, and a newcomer D minor.

WHAT SHALL WE DO WITH THE DRUNKEN SAILOR?

What shall we do with the drunk-en sail-or? What shall we do with the drunken sail-or?
What shall we do with the drunk-en sail-or ear-ly in the morn-ing.
Heigh, ho and up she ris-es, Heigh, ho and up she ris-es,
Heigh, ho and up she ris-es, ear-ly in the morn-ing.

THE MINOR TONALITY

'Hear' the minor key by learning shapes for Em and B7, and strum the chord sequence giving three or four strums to each chord whilst keeping the time regular.

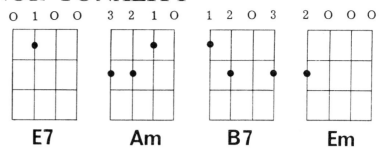

ASH GROVE

The ash grove how grace-ful, how plain-ly 'tis speak-ing, The
G · · · · · G · · Am · · D7

wind through it play-ing, Has lang-uage for me. The
G · · · · C · · G D7 G

friends of my child-hood a-gain are be-fore me, Fond
G · · Am · · D7 · · G

mem-or-ies wak-en, As free-ly I roam. With
Em · · · · · D A7 D

soft whis-pers lad-en, The leaves rus-tle o'er me, The
G · · Em · · Am · · D7

ash grove, the ash grove that shel-tered my home.
G · · · C · · G D7 G

DOWN IN DEMERARA

There was a man who had a hors-e-lum, had a hors-e-lum, had a hors-e-lum,
G - - C G - - - Am - D7 - G - - -

Was a man who had a hors-e-lum, Down in Dem-e-ra-ra, And
G - - C G - - - Am - D7 G - -

Chorus
here we sit like birds in the wil-der-ness, birds in the wil-der-ness, birds in the wil-der-ness,
G - - C G - - - Am - D7 - G - - -

Here we sit like birds in the wil-der-ness, Down in Dem-e-ra-ra.
G - - C G - - - Am - D7 - G - -

26

ROUND HER NECK SHE WORE A GOLDEN LOCKET

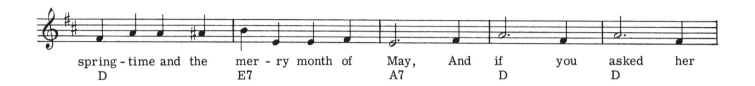

Round her neck she wore a gold-en lock-et, She wore it in the
D   D   D   D   D

spring-time and the mer-ry month of May, And if you asked her
D   E7   A7   D   D

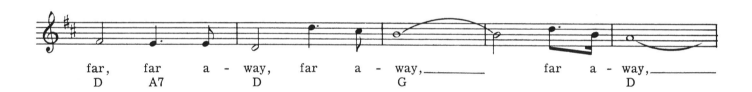

why she wore the lock-et, She wore it for her lov-er who was
D   D   D   D

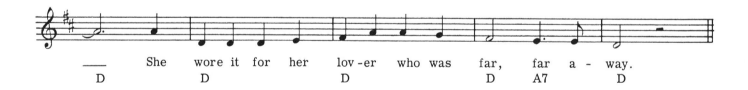

far, far a - way, far a - way,_____ far a - way,_____
D A7 D   G   D

____ She wore it for her lov-er who was far, far a - way.
D   D   D   D A7 D

MICHAEL FINNIGIN

There was an old man called Michael Fin-ni-gin, He grew whis-kers on his chin-i-gin,The
G   G   G   G   Am   Am   D7   D7

wind came up and blew them in-i-gin, Poor old Mich-ael Fin-ni-gin. Be-gin a-gin. There
G   G   G   G   Am   D7   G   G

USEFUL CHORDS FOR GUITAR

Bracketed chords are for four string strum. Develop right hand picking style and play bass notes with the thumb.

Strings marked (X) are not played.

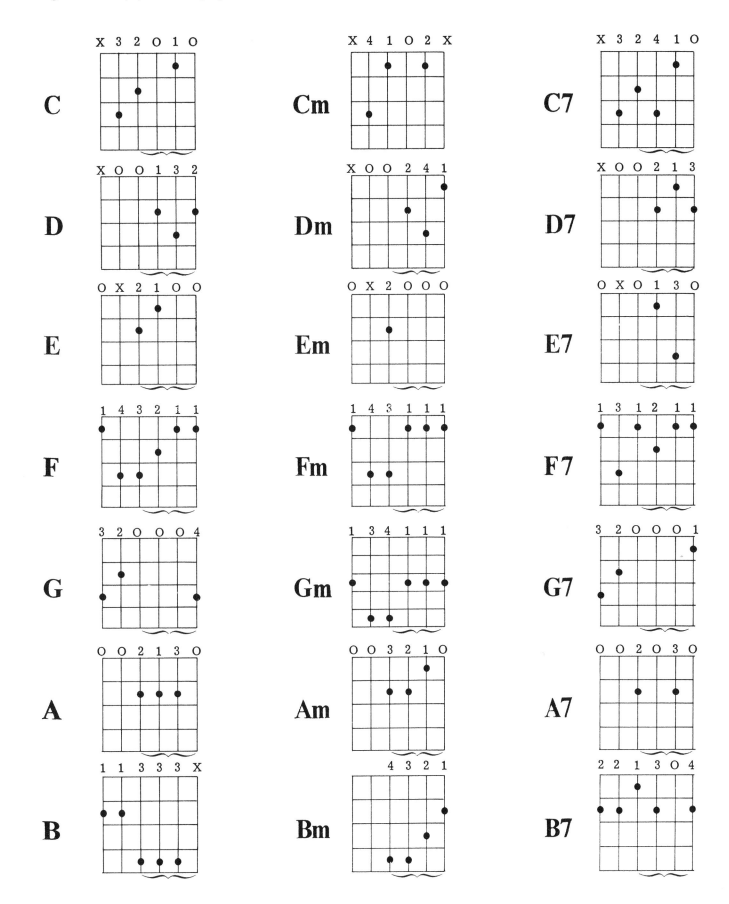

USEFUL CHORDS FOR FIVE STRING BANJO

Chords shown are on the first four strings. The fifth open G string is principally used for arpeggio rolling style or chords which contain the note G natural.

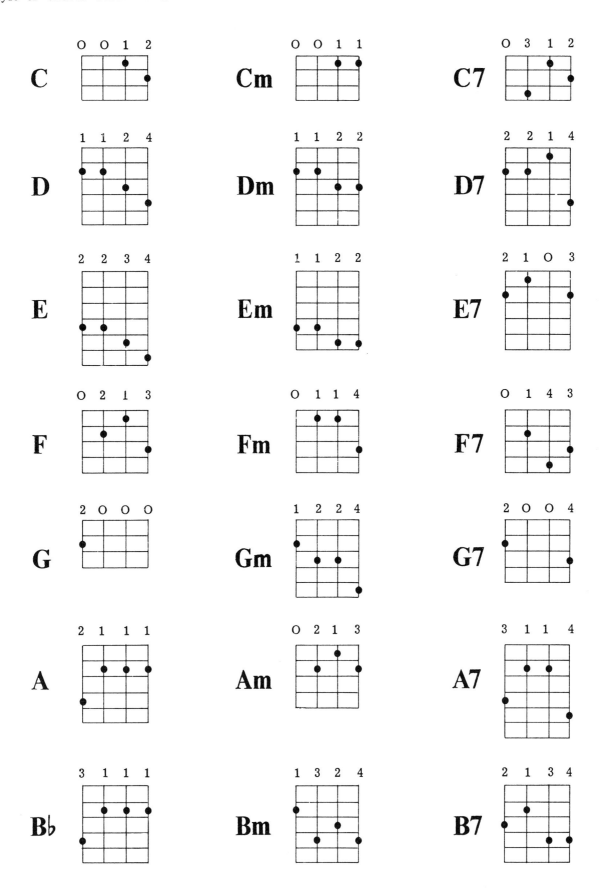

Printed by Halstan & Co. Ltd., Amersham, Bucks., England